Andrew Shitov

Raku One-Liners

Getting the most of Raku's expressive syntax for your daily routines

DeepText — 2019

Raku One-Liners

Getting the most of Raku's expressive syntax for your daily routines
© Andrew Shitov, author, 2019

In this book, you will find a lot of short programs, so short that they can be written in a single line of code. The seven chapters will guide you through Raku's syntax elements that help to create short, expressive, but still useful programs.

It is assumed that the reader knows the basics of the Raku programming language and understands programming in general.

Published on 18 October 2019

Published by DeepText, Amsterdam
www.deeptext.media

ISBN 978-90-821568-9-8

Contents

Chapter 3
Working with Numbers

Chapter 4
Working with Strings

Chapter 5
Working with Dates

Chapter 6
Raku Syntax

Chapter 7
Raku Golf

Preface

Dear reader,

You are reading a book about the Raku programming language. This language has appeared as a rename of the Perl 6 in October 2019.

Like its parent, Perl 5, the Raku language keeps the spirit of being a powerful tool in many areas, from devops programs for configuration management trough different command-line applications to concurrent web servers.

In this book, you will find a number of short programs that you may want to use in your daily practice. You will also find a number of one-line snippets that can enter your bigger programs.

The goal of the book is not to give a copy-and-paste list of coding examples, but to explain the various bits of the Raku language that help to use it more efficiently.

To run the program examples from the rest of the book, you need to download and install the most recent Rakudo Star compiler pack from its website, rakudo.org. If you are using the previous, Perl 6-based compiler, create an alias in your `.profile` file so that you can use the `raku` command to run the compiler:

```
alias raku=perl6
```

I wish you a pleasant journey with the magical Raku language.

Andrew Shitov
Amsterdam, 18 October 2019

Chapter 1
Command-Line Options

Using command-line options

Let us talk about the command-line options that the Rakudo[1] compiler offers to us.

-e

The first option to know when working with Raku is `-e`. It takes a string with your Raku one-liner and executes it immediately.

For example, print the name of the current user:

```
$ raku -e'say $*USER'

ash
```

-n

This option repeats the code for each line of input data. This is quite handy when you want to process a file. For example, here's a one-liner that adds up the values in a row and prints the sum:

```
$ raku -ne'say [+] .split(" ")' data.txt
```

If the `data.txt` file contains the following:

```
10 20 30 40
1 2 3 4
5 6 7 8
```

---

[1] Rakudo (rakudo.org) is an implementation of Raku. The rest of the book assumes you are using the Rakudo compiler and run it as `raku` from command line. If you have an older version, which has the `perl6` executable, make an alias in your `.profile`: `alias raku=perl6`.

then the result of the one-liner is:

```
100
10
26
```

There's no difference whether you use shell's input redirection or not; the following line also works:

```
$ raku -ne'say [+] .split(" ")' < data.txt
```

Make sure you place the e option the last in the list (so, not raku -en'...') or split the options: raku -n -e'...'.

-p

This option is similar to -n but prints the topic variable after each iteration.

The following one-liner reverses the lines in the file and prints them to the console:

```
$ raku -npe'.=flip' data.txt
```

For the same input file, the result will look like this:

```
04 03 02 01
4 3 2 1
8 7 6 5
```

Notice that you have to update the $_ variable, so you type .=flip. If you only have .flip, you will reverse the string, but the result is not used and the *original* line is printed.

An equivalent program with .flip and with no -p looks like this:

```
$ raku -ne'.flip.say' data.txt
```

Examples of short one-lines

Let's go through a few one-liners for working with file as an appetiser. The whole next chapter is devoted to working with files.

Double-space a file

```
$ raku -npe's/$/\n/' text.txt
```

Remove all blank lines

```
$ raku -ne'.say if .chars' text.txt
```

Depending on how you define 'blank', you may want another one-liner that skips the lines containing whitespaces:

```
$ raku -ne'.say if /\S/' text.txt
```

Number all lines in a file

```
$ raku -ne'say ++$ ~ ". " ~ $_' text.txt
```

This code, probably, requires a comment. The $ variable is a *state* variable and it can be used without declaration.

Convert all text to uppercase

```
$ raku -npe'.=uc' text.txt
```

Strip whitespace from the beginning and end of each line

```
$ raku -npe'.=trim' text.txt
```

Print the first line of a file

```
$ raku -ne'.say ; exit' text.txt
```

Print the first 10 lines of a file

```
$ raku -npe'exit if $++ == 10' text.txt
```

This time, the postfix ++ operator was applied to the $ variable.

Reading files with $*ARGFILES

$*ARGFILES is a built-in dynamic variable that may be handy when working with multiple input files.

How do you read two or more files passed in the command line?

```
$ raku work.pl a.txt b.txt
```

If you need to process all files together as if they would be a single data source, you could ask the variable to do the job in a one-liner:

```
.say for $*ARGFILES.lines
```

Inside the program, you don't have to think about looping over the files; $*ARGFILES will automatically do that for you.

If there are no files in the command line, the variable will be attached to STDIN:

```
$ cat a.txt b.txt | raku work.pl
```

Handy indeed, isn't it?

$*ARGFILES and MAIN

I also have to warn you if you will want to use the $*ARGFILES variable in bigger programs. Consider the following example:

```
sub MAIN(*@files) {
    .say for $*ARGFILES.lines;
}
```

In the recent versions of Raku, $*ARGFILES works differently *inside* the MAIN subroutine and *outside* of it.

This program will perfectly work with the earlier versions (before and including Rakudo version 2018.10). Starting from Rakudo Star 2018.12, $*ARGFILES, if used inside MAIN, is always connected to $*IN.

Chapter 2
Working with Files

Renaming files

Let us solve a task to rename all the files passed in the command-line arguments and give the files sequential numbers in the preferred format. Here is an example of the command line:

```
$ raku rename.raku *.jpg img_0000.jpg
```

In this example, all image files in the current directory will be renamed to img_0001.jpg, img_0002.jpg, etc.

And here's the possible solution in Raku (save it in the `rename.raku` file):

```
@*ARGS[0..*-2].sort.map: *.Str.IO.rename(++@*ARGS[*-1])
```

The pre-defined dynamic variable `@*ARGS` contains the arguments from the command line. In the above example, the shell unrolls the `*.jpg` mask to a list of files, so the array contains them all. The last element is the renaming sample img_0000.jpg.

If you are familiar with C or Perl, notice that the variable is called `ARGS`, not ~~ARGV~~.

To loop over all the files (and skipping the last file item with the file mask), we are taking the slice of `@*ARGS`. The `0..*-2` construct creates a range of indices to take all elements except the last one.

Then the list is sorted (the original `@*ARGS` array stays unchanged), and we iterate over the file names using the `map` method.

The body of `map` contains a `WhateveCode` block (see Chapter 6); it takes the string representation of the current value, makes an `IO::Path` object out of it, and calls the `rename` method. Notice that the `IO` method creates an object of the `IO::Path` class; while a bare `IO` is a *role* in the hierarchy of the Raku object system.

Finally, the increment operator `++` changes the renaming sample (which is held in the last, `*-1`st, element of `@*ARGS`). When the operator is applied to a string, it increments the number part of it, so we get img_0001.jpg, img_0002.jpg, etc.

Merging files horizontally

Let us merge a few files into a single file. The task is to take two (or three, or more) files and copy their contents line by line. For example, we want to merge two log files, knowing that all their lines correspond to each other.

File a.txt:

```
2019/12/20 11:16:13
2019/12/20 11:17:58
2019/12/20 11:19:18
2019/12/20 11:24:30
```

File b.txt:

```
"/favicon.ico" failed (No such file)
"/favicon.ico" failed (No such file)
"/robots.txt" failed (No such file)
"/robots.txt" failed (No such file)
```

The first one-liner illustrates the idea:

```
.say for [Z~] @*ARGS.map: *.IO.lines;
```

It is assumed that the program is run as follows:

```
$ raku merge.raku a.txt b.txt
```

For each filename (@*.ARGS.map) in the command line, an IO::Path object
is created (.IO), and the lines from the files are read (.lines).

In the case of two files, we have two sequences, which are then concatenated
line by line using the **zip** meta-operator Z applied to a concatenation infix ~.

After that step, we get another sequence, which we can print line by line
(.say for).

```
2019/12/20 11:16:13"/favicon.ico" failed (No such file)
2019/12/20 11:17:58"/favicon.ico" failed (No such file)
2019/12/20 11:19:18"/robots.txt" failed (No such file)
2019/12/20 11:24:30"/robots.txt" failed (No such file)
```

The result is formally correct, but let's add a space between the original lines.
Here is an updated version of the one-liner:

```
.trim.say for [Z~] @*ARGS.map: *.IO.lines.map: *~ ' '
```

Here, a space character is appended to the end of each line (.map: *~ ' '),
and as there will be one extra space at the end of the combined line, it is
removed by the trim method. Its sibling, trim-trailing, could be used instead (or a regex if you care about original trailing spaces happened to be in
the second file).

With the above change, the files are perfectly merged now:

```
2019/12/20 11:16:13 "/favicon.ico" failed (No such file)
2019/12/20 11:17:58 "/favicon.ico" failed (No such file)
2019/12/20 11:19:18 "/robots.txt" failed (No such file)
2019/12/20 11:24:30 "/robots.txt" failed (No such file)
```

There's no problem to merge the same file to itself, or to provide more than
two files, for example:

```
$ raku merge.raku a.txt a.txt a.txt
```

Reversing a file

In this section, we are creating a one-liner to print the lines of a text file in reversed order (as `tail -r` does it).

The first one-liner does the job with the STDIN stream:

```
.say for $*IN.lines.reverse
```

Run the program as:

```
$ raku reverse.raku < text.txt
```

`$*IN` can be omitted in this case, which makes the one-liner even shorter:

```
.say for lines.reverse
```

If you want to read the files directly from Raku, modify the program a bit to create a file handle out of the command-line argument:

```
.say for @*ARGS[0].IO.open.lines.reverse
```

Now you run it as follows:

```
$ raku reverse.raku text.txt
```

It is important to remember that the default behaviour of the `lines` method is to exclude the newline characters from the final sequence of lines (the method returns a `Seq` object, not an array or a list).

In Raku, the `lines` method splits the lines based on the value stored in the `.nl-in` attribute of the `IO::Handle` object.

You can look at the current value of the line separators with the following tiny script:

```
dd $_ for @*ARGS[0].IO.open.nl-in
```

This is what you find there by default:

```
$["\n", "\r\n"]
```

The interesting thing is that you can control the behaviour of `lines` and tell Raku not to exclude the newline characters:

```
@*ARGS[0].IO.open(chomp => False).lines.reverse.put
```

The `chomp` attribute is set to `True` by default. You can also change the default separator:

```
@*ARGS[0].IO.open(
    nl-in => "\r", chomp => False
).lines.reverse.put
```

Notice that without chomping, you do not need an explicit `for` loop over the lines: in the last two one-liners, the `.put` method is called directly on the sequence object. In the earlier versions, the strings did not contain the newline characters, and thus they would be printed as a single long line.

A small homework for you: *Tell the difference between* `put` *and* `say`.

Chapter 3
Working with Numbers

Grepping dividable numbers

The task is to find the sum of all multiples of 3 and 5 below 1000. The first elements of the row of our interest are 3, 5, 9, 15, 20, 21, etc. You can already see that some of them, such as 15, are multiples of both 3 and 5, so it is not possible to add up multiples of 3 and 5 separately.

The short story is here:

```
say sum((1..999).grep: * %% (3 | 5))
```

Now, let us decipher it.

What we need is to filter the numbers that are multiples of either 3 or 5. If you re-read the previous sentence, a bell should ring for you: in Raku, this can be achieved with **junctions**, informally known as quantum superpositions. To test if a number is dividable by either 3 or 5, write the following:

```
$x %% 3 | 5
```

By the way, %%, the divisibility operator, is a very sweet thing that helps avoiding negations in Boolean tests, which you would have written as follows, would you only have a single percent:

```
!($x % (3 | 5))
```

OK, the main condition is ready, let us scan the numbers between 1 and (including) 999:

```
(1..999).grep: * %% (3 | 5)
```

A few more interesting language elements appear here. For example, the `WhateverCode` block, which was introduced by a * character (see Chapter 6). Together with the colon-form of method calls, it allows to get rid of a nested pair of braces and parentheses. Without the *, the code would be more complicated:

```
(1..999).grep({$_ %% (3 | 5)})
```

The numbers are filtered (*grepped* if you prefer), and it's time to add them up and print the result. We come to the final one-liner shown at the beginning of this section.

Of course, instead of writing `say sum(...)` one could do a method call or two:

```
((1..999).grep: * %% (3 | 5)).sum.say
```

As a bonus track, here's my first solution, which is much longer than a one-liner:

```
sub f($n) {
    ($n <<*>> (1...1000 / $n)).grep: * < 1000
}

say (f(3) ∪ f(5)).keys.sum;
```

Generating random integers

You may ask, what's the deal with it, isn't it a routine task to call a kind of a rand unction? Well, in some sense, yes, but you might prefer calling a *method*.

Let's look at the following code:

```
2020.rand.Int.say;
```

That's the whole program, and it generates random numbers below 2020. It only uses method calls, chained one after another. If you have never seen Raku before, the first thing you notice here is a method called on a number. That's not something extraordinary in this language.

Calling the `rand` method on a number is potentially a call of the method defined in the `Cool` class, which is immediately delegated to a numeric representation of the number:

```
method rand() { self.Num.rand }
```

Later in the `Num` class, a call to the underlying NQP engine happens:

```
method rand(Num:D: ) {
    nqp::p6box_n(nqp::rand_n(nqp::unbox_n(self)));
}
```

In our example, the object `2020` is an `Int`, so `rand` is dispatched directly to the method of the `Num` class.

The `rand` method returns a floating-point number, so call another method, `Int`, on it to get an integer.

Run the code a few times to confirm that it generates random numbers:

```
$ raku -e'2020.rand.Int.say'
543
$ raku -e'2020.rand.Int.say'
1366
$ raku -e'2020.rand.Int.say'
1870
```

If you want to understand the quality of the random number generator, dig deeper to NQP and MoarVM, and later to the backend engine of the virtual machine. To make the results repeatable (e. g., for tests), set the seed by calling the `srand` function:

```
$ raku -e'srand(10); 2020.rand.Int.say'
296
$ raku -e'srand(10); 2020.rand.Int.say'
296
```

Notice that the srand routine is a *subroutine*, not a method. It is also defined in the same Num class:

```
proto sub srand($, *%) {*}
multi sub srand(Int:D $seed --> Int:D) {
    nqp::p6box_i(nqp::srand($seed))
}
```

And if you have the chance to see the source file, you would most likely notice that there's also a standalone subroutine for rand:

```
proto sub rand(*%) {*}
multi sub rand(--> Num:D) {
    nqp::p6box_n(nqp::rand_n(1e0))
}
```

You can only call it without arguments, in which case Raku generates a random number between 0 and 1. Would you pass the argument, you'll get an error explaining that a method call is preferable:

```
$ raku -e'rand(20)'
===SORRY!=== Error while compiling -e
Unsupported use of rand(N); in Raku please use N.rand for Num
or (^N).pick for Int result
at -e:1
------> rand⏏(20)
```

Working with big numbers

In this section, we'll look at the Problem 13 of Project Euler. Let me show a part of it:

```
37107287533902102798797998220837590246510135740250
46376937677490009712648124896970078050417018260538
743249861995247410594742333309513058123726617309629
91942213363574161572522430563301811072406154908250
23067588207539346171171980310421047513778063246676
89261670696623633820136378418383684178734361726757
28112879812849979408065481931592621691275889832738
44274228917432520321923589422876796487670272189318
47451445736001306439091167216856844588711603153276
70386486105843025439939619828917593665686757934951
62176457141856560629502157223196586755079324193331
64906352462741904929101432445813822663347944758178
92575867718337217661963751590579239728245598838407
58203565325359399008402633568948830189458628227828
80181199384826282014278194139940567587151170094390
35398664372827112653829987240784473053190104293586
86515506006295864861532075273371959191420517255829
71693888707715466499115593487603532921714970056938
54370070576826684624621495650076471787294438377604
53282654108756828443191190634694037855217779295145
36123272525000296071075082563815656710885258350721
45876576172410976447339110607218265236877223636045
17423706905851860660448207621209813287860733969412
81142660418086830619328460811191061556940512689692
```

. . .

```
72107838435069186155435662884062257473692284509516
20849603980134001723930671666823555245252804609722
53503534226472524250874054075591789781264330331690
```

Indeed, the number looks huge, and the task is to find the first ten digits of the sum of a hundred integers, each consisting of 50 digits.

Sounds like a task that may require some optimisation and simplification to get rid of everything which does not contribute to the first ten digits of the result. But not in Raku.

Here, you can simply add up the numbers and take the first ten digits of it:

```
  <
    3710728743390210279879799822083759024651013574025 0
    # Other 98 numbers here
    5350353452647252425087405407559178978126433033169 0
  >.sum.substr(0, 10).say
```

Raku is operating with arbitrary-long integers by default; you don't need to include any modules or somehow else activate this behaviour. You can even calculate powers and get the result quickly enough:

```
$ raku -e'say 3710728743390210279879799822083759 0 ** 1000'
```

Another thing to notice is that we can transparently cast strings to numbers and vice versa. In the current program, the list of numbers is presented as a quoted list of strings within a pair of angle brackets.

On the list, you call the `sum` method, which works with numbers. After getting the sum, you treat it as a string again and extract the first ten characters of it. The whole code looks very natural and it is easy to read.

Testing palindromic numbers

The task is to find the largest palindromic number (the number that reads from both ends, such as 1551), which is a product of two three-digit numbers.

In other words, we have to scan the numbers below 999×999, and could optimise the solution, but in reality, we only have to allow numbers, which are products, thus, let's not skip the multiplication part.

Here's our one-liner:

```
(((999...100) X* (999...100)).grep: {$^a eq $^a.flip}).max.say
```

You are already prepared to the fact that chained method calls are very handy for using in Raku one-liners.

We also saw the colon-form of method calls earlier, but this time we are using a code block with a *placeholder* variable. It is not quite clear if you can use a star here, as we need the variable twice in the block.

The first part of the line uses the cross-operator `X*`, (see Chapter 6). It generates products of all three-digit numbers. As we need the largest number, it makes sense to start from right to left, that's why the sequence `999...100`, but not `100...999`.

Let's look at the first few numbers in the grepped sequence of products:

```
580085 514415 906609 119911 282282 141141 853358 650056
```

One-liners are not always very optimal. In our case, we need to generate the whole sequence of products to find the maximum among them. The answer resides at the third position, so it will be a mistake to replace `max` with `first`. But the good part is that if you use `first`, Raku will not generate all the numbers. There's another useful method, `head`, which also prevents generating more than necessary.

The following code runs much faster and gives the correct result:

```
(((999...100) X* (999...100)).grep:
    {$^a eq $^a.flip}).head(10).max.say
```

Adding up even Fibonacci numbers

The task here is to find the sum of all even Fibonacci numbers below four million.

Here's the complete solution:

```
(1, 1, * + * ... * >= 4_000_000).grep(* %% 2).sum.say
```

It is equally interesting to parse the code from either left or right end. Let's start from left.

Inside the first parentheses, we are generating a sequence of Fibonacci numbers, which starts with two 1s, and each next generated number is a sum of the two previous ones. You can express it using a `WhateverCode` block: `* + *` is equivalent to `{$^a + $^b}`.

A less known feature of sequences is the final condition. In many examples you would see either a bare star or an `Inf`. In our example, we limit the sequence with an explicit upper boundary.

Notice that you cannot simply write:

```
1, 1, * + * ... 4_000_000
```

To visualise it better, try a smaller limit, say 100:

```
> (1, 1, * + * ... 100)
(1 1 2 3 5 8 13 21 34 55 89 144 233 377 610 987 1597 2584
4181
```

The generation does not stop when the sequence crosses our desired border. It will only stop it if the next calculated element of the sequence equals to the given number exactly, for example:

```
> (1, 1, * + * ... 144)
(1 1 2 3 5 8 13 21 34 55 89 144)
```

If you don't know the Fibonacci number preceding four million, use another WhateverCode block with a Boolean condition: `* >= 4_000_000`. Notice that the condition is opposite to what you would write in a regular loop, as here we are demanding *more than four million*, not *less than*. This is the condition that becomes `True` when you have to stop the sequence. Without the star, you could use the default variable: `{$_ >= 4_000_000}`.

The rest of the code greps even numbers and adds them up.

Playing with Fibonacci numbers

Yes, most likely, you never used such numbers in real code, and, again, most likely, you solved many educating problems with them. Nevertheless, today, let's try to approach the shortest solution for a Fibonacci problem on the Code-Golf.io site (see also Chapter 7 about Golf coding).

How do we form a Fibonacci sequence? With a sequential operator ...:

```
0, 1, * + * ... *
```

If you want some exotic flavour in the code, you can replace the last star with either `Inf` or ∞. In any case, the result is a lazy sequence of the `Seq` type. Raku does not compute it immediately (and it can't, as the right edge is infinite).

Finally, let's find the index of the first Fibonacci number, which has 1000 digits. Of course, you can loop over the above-created sequence and trace the index yourself. But in Raku, there is an option to modify the `grep` routine family and ask it to return the index of the matched item instead of the item itself.

Also, instead of `grep`, we'll use a more appropriate method, `first`. It returns the first matching item or its index if we call the method with the k key. It is enough just to mention the key; no value is really needed.

```
say (0, 1, * + * ... *).first(*.chars >= 1000, :k)
```

This program prints a single integer number, which is the correct answer to the given problem.

Distance between two points

Here's an illustration to help to formulate the task. Our goal is to find the distance between the points A and B.

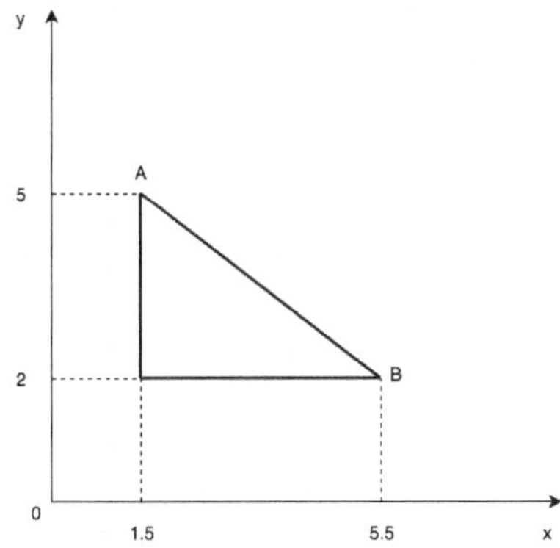

To make the answer more transparent and easier to check, I chose the line AB so that it is a hypotenuse of a right triangle with the sides of length 3 and 4. The length of the third side is 5 in this case.

Here's the solution:

```
say abs(5.5+2i - (1.5+5i))
```

The code uses complex numbers, and as soon as you move the problem to a complex plane, you gain from the fact that the distance between the two points on the surface equals to the absolute value of subtraction of these two numbers from one another.

One of the points, in this case, is the point $5.5+2i$ on the complex plane, and the second point is $1.5+5i$. In Raku, you write down complex numbers as you do in mathematics.

Without the built-in support of complex numbers, you would have to use Pythagorean theorem explicitly:

```
say sqrt((5.5 - 1.5)² + (2 - 5)²)
```

Homework. *Modify Rakudo's grammar to allow the following code:*

```
say √((5.5 - 1.5)² + (2 - 5)²)
```

Playing with prime numbers

Let us solve the problem where you need to print the 10001st prime number (having the first being 2).

The Raku programming language is good at prime numbers, as it has a built-in method of the `Int` class, `is-prime`.

There are a few ways of generating prime numbers. For one-liners, the best is the simplest, but the least efficient, method that tests every number.

```
say ((1..*).grep: *.is-prime)[10000]
```

It takes about half-a-minute to compute the result, but the code is quite short. Solving the task using the so-called sieve of Eratosthenes is much more efficient, but it probably requires more lines of code, thus it is not a one-liner and is out of scope of this book.

Using map and Seq to compute the value of π

In this section, we are computing the value of π using two different methods. The goal is to try different approaches to generate numeric sequences.

Preparation

Of course, you don't need to calculate the value of π yourself, as the Raku language gives us a few predefined constants in the shape of both π and `pi`, as well as doubled values τ and `tau`.

But to demonstrate the usage of maps and sequences, let's implement one of the simplest algorithms to calculate π:

$$\frac{\pi}{4} = 1 - \frac{1}{3} + \frac{1}{5} - \frac{1}{7} + \dots$$

Here's a draft code to check the answer:

```
my $pi = 1;
my $sign = 1;

for 1..10000 -> $k {
    $sign *= -1;
    $pi += $sign / ($k * 2 + 1);
}

say 4 * $pi;
```

Part 1

Now, let us employ `map` to make the solution compact. It is better to make the formula more generic, too:

$$\pi = 4 \sum_{n=0}^{\infty} \frac{-1^n}{2n + 1}$$

And here's our first one-liner:

```
say 4 * [+] (^1000).map({(-1) ** $_ / (2 * $_ + 1)})
```

I hope you understand everything here. We covered different parts of this solution in the previous sections of the book.

But still, I want to emphasise that you need parentheses around `-1`. If you type `-1 ** $_`, then you always get -1, as the minus prefix is applied to the result of taking power. So, the correct code is `(-1) ** $_`.

Part 2

It is also interesting to try using a sequence operator ... to generate the row according to the formula mentioned above. Also, we'll use rational numbers to create the fractions ⅓, ⅕, etc.

```
say 4 * [+] <1/1>,
    {-Rat.new($^n.numerator, $^n.denominator + 2)} ...
    *.abs < 1E-5;
```

This sequence starts with a rational number `<1/1>`, which is handy as we can immediately take its numerator and denominator. The generator block of the sequence uses this number to create a new rational number, whose denominator increases by two on each iteration.

You may ask why I am referring `$^n.numerator`, which is always 1. This is needed, because to alter the sign, we need to know the sign of the current value, and the sign is kept in the numerator part of the rational value.

The placeholder variable `$^n` automatically takes the first (and the only) argument of the generator code block.

The sequence is generated until the absolute value of the current value becomes small enough. It may be tempting to replace the final condition with `* ≅ 0`, but that program would run too long to produce the result, as the default tolerance of the approximately-equal operator is 10^{-15}, while the row does not converge that fast.

Also, you cannot use the `< ... / ...>` syntax to create a `Rat` number in the generator:

```
{ <$^n.numerator / $^n.denominator + 2> }
```

In this case, Raku treats this as a quoting construction such as `<red green blue>`, and instead of the code block you get a list of strings.

Part 3

Damian Conway suggested the following interesting and compact solution using sequences:

```
say 4 * [+] (1, -1, 1 … *   )
          «/« (1,  3, 5 … 9999);
```

Computing totals

In this section, we'll see a one-liner that calculates totals for the columns of a table.

Here's some sample data in a file:

```
100.20  303.50 150.25
130.44 1505.12  36.41
200.12  305.60  78.12
```

And here's the code that prints three numbers—totals for each column:

```
put [Z+] lines.map: *.words
```

The program prints the numbers that we need:

```
430.76 2114.22 264.78
```

We know that bare `lines` is the same as `$*IN.lines`, so `lines.map` iterates over all the lines in the input stream. Each line is then split into words—substrings separated by whitespaces.

The part of the job that parses input data is complete. We have got a number of sequences corresponding to the lines of input data. For our sample file, these are the following:

```
(("100.20", "303.50", "150.25").Seq, ("130.44", "1505.12",
"36.41").Seq, ("200.12", "305.60", "78.12").Seq).Seq
```

Now, add up every first element, every second element, etc. The combination of the reduction operator and the zip meta-operators does all the work with only four characters: `[Z+]`.

At this point, we have a reduced sequence:

```
(430.76, 2114.22, 264.78).Seq
```

The last trivial step is to print the values using the `put` routine. If you did the homework earlier, you would know that `say` uses the `gist` method (which adds parentheses around a sequence) to visualise the result, while `put` simply prints the values using the `Str` method.

Let us add a few more characters to the script to demonstrate how you can skip the first column that, for example, contains month names:

```
Jan 100.20  303.50 150.25
Feb 130.44 1505.12  36.41
Mar 200.12  305.60  78.12
```

All you need is to make a slice and select all columns except the first one:

```
put 'Total ', [Z+] lines.map: *.words[1..*]
```

As you see, we even don't need to count columns ourselves. The `1..*` range can make that job.

Sum of the numbers equal to the sum of factorials of digits

So, the task is to find the sum of all numbers, which are equal to the sum of factorials of their digits. Sounds clear? You may take a look at the solution one-liner to understand it better.

```
say [+] (3..50_000).grep({$_ == [+] .comb.map({[*] 2..$_})})
```

Let us start from … something.

We are looping over the range 3 .. 50_000. The upper boundary is a guess based on some considerations. I would not be explaining it here, but you may try to find the answer if you are curious. Basically, at some point you understand that the number either contains too many digits or is too big itself.

The second step is to grep. We are searching for the numbers, which are equal ($_ ==) to the sum. It is calculated by the second reduction plus [+], but you may use the sum method instead:

```
{$_ == .comb.map({[*] 2..$_}).sum}
```

Notice that .comb is a method called on the default variable $_. The comb method splits the number to separate the digits (treating them as characters). The map method converts each digit to a factorial (again, using the reduction operator [*]).

Finally, the most outer [+] adds up all the grepped numbers and passes the result to the say routine.

Although the book is about one-liners, it would be more practical to devote a separate line of code to prepare the factorials before using them:

```
my @f = (0..9).map({[*] 1..$_});
say [+] (3..50_000).grep({$_ == [+] .comb.map({@f[$_]})});
```

42 via the cubes

You might have seen the calculation that leads to getting an exact value of *42*, the answer of *Life, the Universe and Everything*. Let me copy it here, using the power of Raku and its arbitrary precision arithmetic, not to mention the pleasure of using superscripts directly in the code.

```
$ time raku -e'say 80435758145817515³ - 80538738812075974³ +
12602123297335631³'

42

real 0m0.151s
user 0m0.173s
sys 0m0.035s
```

Chapter 4
Working with Strings

Generating random passwords

Here's the full code addressing the problem:

```
('0'..'z').pick(15).join.say
```

Run it a few times:

```
Z4x72B8wkWHo0QD
J;V?=CE84jIS^r9
2;m6>kdHRS04XEL
O6wK=umZ]DqyHT5
3SP\tNkX5Zh@1C4
PX6QC?KdWYyzNOc
bq1EfBZNdK9vHxz
```

Our line of code generates different strings each time you run it. Try it your-self to create a password or take one of the above-shown passwords if you did not install Raku yet.

You may also ask a question: *What characters can I expect in the password?* Great that you ask! Raku is a Unicode-oriented language, and the range `'0'..'z'` seems to contain characters with different Unicode properties (i. e., digits and letters at least). To see what's inside, just remove the `pick` method from our today's code:

```
('0'..'z').join.say
```

This line prints the subset of the ASCII table between the two given char-acters:

```
0123456789:;<=>?@
ABCDEFGHIJKLMNOPQRSTUVWXYZ[\]^_`
abcdefghijklmnopqrstuvwxyz
```

These are the characters that may appear in the password. The `pick` method makes sure characters are not repeated. If you use `roll` instead, then you allow occurrence of characters more than once.

The joy of Unicode

The code here is using four characters outside of the ASCII land:

```
say π × $ρ²
```

In Raku, you can freely use the Unicode characters in identifiers, such as variable or function names. But on top of that, there are many pre-defined symbols such as π, which have ASCII alternatives. Examine the documentation page called *'Unicode versus ASCII symbols'* to see the whole set of the Unicode characters that can be used in Raku.

Using ASCII only, the above one-liner can be re-written in the following way:

```
say pi * $r ** 2
```

Let's return to one of the helper programs from the previous chapter and see where Unicode characters could be used:

```
sub f($n) {
    ($n <<*>> (1...1000 / $n)).grep: * < 1000
}


say (f(3) ∪ f(5)).keys.sum;
```

There are a few opportunities here.

First, a hyper-operator <<*>> can be replaced with proper French quotes: «*», and the multiplication character can be a cross that we used already: «×». The same can be applied to division: ÷.

Second, the three dots of the sequence operator are replaceable with a single Unicode character: … (if you are programming in Word, you get this character automatically after typing the full stop three times).

Finally, in the last line, a Unicode character ∪ is used to find the intersection of two sets. The character here is the same that you use in mathematics (do you?), but you can use its ASCII version instead: f(3) (|) f(5).

Unicode support is one of the best if not the best among programming languages. Use it with care not to make other people crazy about your code!

Chapter 5
Working with Dates

What's the date today?

Today, we'll answer the question of what's the date today.

So, to print the answer, you can use the following line of Raku code:

```
DateTime.now.yyyy-mm-dd.say
```

It looks transparent and prints the date in the format of YYYY-MM-DD. The good part is that the `DateTime` class is available straight ahead, and you don't need to import any modules.

```
$ raku -e'DateTime.now.yyyy-mm-dd.say'
2019-10-17
```

As you have already seen in the previous chapters, chained method calls is a common practice in Raku. An opposite alternative would be to use `say` as a subroutine and use parentheses to after the method names:

```
say(DateTime.now().yyyy-mm-dd());
```

This code also works; it is completely correct, but it looks heavy.

What you should also notice and tell your friends, is that in Raku, you can use dashes and apostrophes in identifiers.

Well, maybe using apostrophes is not a great idea, but hyphens are used very widely already in the source code of Rakudo. Just make sure you put spaces around minus operator in arithmetical expressions to avoid any conflicts in parsing.

If you read documentation, you will find another method named in the same manner: `hh-mm-ss`. I bet you understand what it does.

```
> DateTime.now.hh-mm-ss.say
00:12:01
```

Notice that you will not find similar methods for different formats of the output, such as dd-mm-yy or hh-mm. Use the formatter instead. It is not a method, but an attribute defined in the Datish role. There is a default formatter in the DateTime class, but you may redefine it by providing the constructor with your own subroutine, for example:

```
DateTime.now(formatter => -> $dt {
    sprintf '%02d.%02d.%04d',
    $dt.day, $dt.month, $dt.year
}).say
```

A formatter here takes an anonymous subroutine (introduces by an thin arrow) with one argument $dt.

I hope this code prints the same date as our initial one-liner, as you most likely read the whole section within one day.

How many days in the century match the condition?

Our next one-liner is quite long, and it would be better to write it in two lines, but it will show a very nice feature of Raku's Date objects: it can be easily used in a range.

In essence, the task is to count Sundays between 1 January 1901 and 31 December 2000, and only count Sundays that fall on the first of the months.

The Date object in Raku implements the succ and prec methods, which are used to increment and decrement the date. It is also possible to use two dates as the boundaries of a range:

```
say (
    Date.new(year => 1901) ..^ Date.new(year => 2001)
).grep({.day == 1 && .day-of-week == 7}).elems
```

There are a few moments to comment here.

First, the two `Date` objects are created with a single named parameter, the `year`. This is possible because the signature of the constructor includes default values for both the month and the day:

```
multi method new(
    Date: Int:D() :$year!,
    Int:D() :$month = 1, Int:D() :$day = 1,
    :&formatter, *%_) {
    . . .
}
```

So, it's easy to create a date for 1 January, but you can't do that for the last day of the year. But Raku has a nice range operator `..^`, which excludes the right boundary and allows us to save quite a few characters (while we are not playing Raku Golf yet, that's the topic of Chapter 7).

The longer version, with all explicit parts of the dates, would then look like this:

```
say (
    Date.new(year => 1901, month => 1, day => 1) ..
    Date.new(year => 2000, month => 12, day => 31)
).grep({.day == 1 && .day-of-week == 7}).elems
```

You create a range and grep its values using a combined condition. Remember that there is no need to explicitly type `$_` when you want to call a method on the default variable.

An alternative would be to use two greps with a star:

```
say (
    Date.new(year => 1901, month => 1, day => 1) ..
    Date.new(year => 2000, month => 12, day => 31)
).grep(*.day == 1).grep(*.day-of-week == 7).elems
```

An exercise for you to make at home: *Print the number of days left until the end of the current year.*

Another solution of the same problem

Here is another solution of the **problem**. The task was to count all Sundays that fall on the first of the month in the XX century.

Last time, we just were scanning through all the days in the whole century, selecting the ones that are Sundays (`.day-of-week == 7`) and are the first of the month (`.day == 1`).

It is possible to make a more efficient algorithm. As we are only interested in the first days of the month, there is no need to scan all 36525 days for 100 years. Only 1200 days that are the first day of each month between 1901 and 2000 are enough.

So, we need two nested loops: over the years and over the months. Do we need two `for`s? Not necessarily. Let's use the `X` operator (see Chapter 6 for more details on it).

And here is our new one-liner:

```
(gather for 1901..2000 X 1..12 {
    take Date.new(|@_, 1)
}).grep(*.day-of-week == 7).elems.say;
```

The `for 1901..2000 X 1..12` loop goes over each month in the XX century. For each, we create a `Date` object by calling a constructor with three arguments.

Notice that inside the loop, you can use both `$_[0]` and `$_[1]`, and `@_[0]` and `@_[1]`. In the first case, the `$_` variable contains a list of two elements, while it is an array `@_` in the second one. The shortest code is achieved if you are just using a dot to call a method on the topic (default) variable: `.[0]` and `.[1]`.

Instead of `Date.new(|@_, 1)`, you can type `Date.new(.[0], .[1], 1)`. The `|@_` syntax is used to unroll the array, as otherwise Raku will think you are passing an array as a first argument.

All first days of the months are collected in a sequence with the help of the `gather`—`take` pair.

The final step is a `grep` as before, but this time we only need to select Sundays, so a single `*.day-of-week == 7` condition is enough.

The call of the `elems` method returns the number of the elements in the list, which is the number of Sundays that we are looking for. Thus, print it with `say`.

Based on a very relevant comment from the reader, here's even better and simpler way of the solution, where the + prefix operator is used to cast a list to its length:

```
say +(1901..2000 X 1..12).map(
    {Date.new(|@_, 1)}
).grep(*.day-of-week == 7);
```

Chapter 6
Raku Syntax

More on X, .., and ...

In the previous chapters, we often used a construct with a cross-operator. Here are a couple of examples:

```
(999...100) X* (999...100)

1..10 X* 1..10
```

The second line prints the items of the product table for the numbers from 1 to 10:

```
(1 2 3 4 5 6 7 8 9 10 2 4 6 8 10 12 14 16 18 20 3 6 9 12 15
18 21 24 27 30 4 8 12 16 20 24 28 32 36 40 5 10 15 20 25 30
35 40 45 50 6 12 18 24 30 36 42 48 54 60 7 14 21 28 35 42 49
56 63 70 8 16 24 32 40 48 56 64 72 80 9 18 27 36 45 54 63 72
81 90 10 20 30 40 50 60 70 80 90 100)
```

There are a few things to learn about such constructions.

You may have noticed two subtle differences between `999...100` and `1..10`. In one case, there are three dots, in another—only two. In the first case, the boundaries are decreasing numbers, in the second—increasing.

The two dots in Raku is the range operator. It creates a `Range`, or, in other words, an object of the `Range` type.

The three dots are the sequence operator. In our example, it creates a sequence, or an object of the `Seq` type.

You can always check the type by calling the `WHAT` method on the object (a fragment of the REPL session is shown below):

```
> (1..10).WHAT
(Range)
```

```
> (1...10).WHAT
(Seq)
```

It is also interesting to look into the source codes of Rakudo, and see which attributes the `Range` and `Seq` have.

```
my class Range is Cool does Iterable does Positional {
    has $.min;
    has $.max;
    has int $!excludes-min;
    has int $!excludes-max;
    has int $!infinite;
    has int $!is-int;

    . . .
}


my class Seq is Cool does Iterable does Sequence {
    has Iterator $!iter;

    . . .
}
```

In the `Range` object, there are the minimum and the maximum values, while in `Seq` we see an iterator.

In some cases, for example, in a simple loop, you can choose between either a range or a sequence:

```
.say for 1..10;
.say for 1...10;
```

But if you want to count downwards, ranges will not work:

```
> .say for 10..1;
Nil
```

With a sequence, there's no problem:

```
> .print for 10...1;
10987654321>
```

It is wise to play with ranges and sequences before you start feeling them well. Save them in variables, use in operations, print using **say** or dd.

As a starting point, consider the following three operations:

```
(1, 2, 3) X* (4, 5, 6);
(1..3)    X* (4..6);
(1...3)   X* (4...6);
```

Reduction operator

Our next guest is a reduction construction with a pair of square brackets. When they do not surround an array index, they work in a completely different field.

Example 1: factorial

The most classical example is using the reduction operator to calculate factorial:

```
say [*] 1..2019
```

[ ] is a **reduction meta-operator**. The *meta* part of the name tells us that it can be used as an envelope for another operator (and not only an operator, by the way).

In the first example, the operator includes another operator, and the whole line can be re-written by enrolling the range to a list and placing the * between all its elements:

```
say 1 * 2 * 3 #`(more elements) * 2018 * 2019
```

Example 2: using a function

Now, let us find the smallest number, which is dividable by all numbers from 1 to 20.

Let me show you a direct answer in Raku:

```
say [lcm] 1..20
```

This code looks very similar to the previous example, but uses another operator, the `lcm` routine, which is a built-in infix operator. The name stands for *least common multiplier*, but in the documentation, you can also read that it returns *the smallest integer that is evenly divisible by both arguments*. Almost the same words, which were used to formulate the problem we solve.

```
say 1 lcm 2 lcm 3 lcm 4 lcm 5 lcm 6 lcm 7 # ... and up to 20
```

Example 3: matrices

Other infix operators that are already built-in in Raku, can also be very productive. Here's an example of rotating a matrix with just a few characters of code:

```
[Z] <A B C>, <D E F>, <H I J>
```

Here, we are transforming a two-dimensional matrix with nine elements, the one-character strings A through J. In the output, the rows become columns, and columns become rows:

```
((A D H) (B E I) (C F J))
```

The zip infix operator `Z` has been inserted between the elements of the list, and thus the code is similar to the following:

```
<A B C> Z <D E F> Z <H I J>
```

Notice, that if you want to emphasise the order of operations, you might get not exactly what you wanted:

```
> (<A B C> Z <D E F>) Z <H I J>
(((A D) H) ((B E) I) ((C F) J))
```

OK, before we did not go too far towards Lisp, let's change the topic.

All the stars of Raku

In this section, we go through the constructs that employ the * character. In Raku you may call it a *star* (or *asterisk* if you prefer) or a *whatever*, depending on the context.

Raku is not a cryptic programming language. On the other side, some areas require spending time to start feeling confident in the syntax.

Let's go through different use cases of *, starting with the simplest, and aiming to understand the most brain-breaking ones such as * ** *.

The first couple of usages is simple and does not require many comments:

Multiplication operator

A single star is used for multiplication. Strictly speaking, this is an infix operator `infix:`, whose return value is `Numeric`.

```
say 20 * 18; # 360
```

Exponentiation operator

The double star ** is the exponentiation operator. Again, this is an `infix:`
that returns the `Numeric` result, calculating the power for the given two values.

```
say pi ** e; # 22.4591577183611
```

A regex repetition quantifier

The same two tokens, * or **, are also used in regexes, where they mean
different things. One of the features of Raku is that it can easily switch between different sub-languages inside itself. Both regexes and grammars are
examples of such inner languages, where the same symbols can mean different things from what they mean in the 'main' language (if they have any
meaning at all there).

The * quantifier. This syntax item works similarly to its behaviour in general
Perl-compatible regexes: allows zero or more repetitions of the atom.

```
my $weather = '*****';
my $snow = $weather ~~ / ('*'*) /;

say 'Snow level is ' ~ $snow.chars; # Snow level is 5
```

Of course, we also see here another usage of the same character, the `'*'`
literal.

Min to max repetitions

The double ** is a part of another quantifier that specifies the minimum
and the maximum number of repetitions:

```
my $operator = '..';
```

```
say "'$operator' is a valid Raku operator"
    if $operator ~~ /^ '.' ** 1..3 $/;
```

In this example, it is expected that the dot is repeated one, two, or three times; not less and not more.

Let's look a bit ahead, and use a star in the role (role as in theatre, not in Raku's object-oriented programming) of the `Whatever` symbol:

```
my $phrase = 'I love you......';

say 'You are so uncertain...'
    if $phrase ~~ / '.' ** 4..* /;
```

The second end of the range is open, and the regex accepts all the phrases with more than four dots in it.

Slurpy arguments

A star before an array argument in a sub's signature means a *slurpy* argument—the one that consumes separate scalar parameters into a single array.

```
list-gifts('chocolade', 'ipad', 'camelia', 'raku');

sub list-gifts(*@items) {
    say 'Look at my gifts this year:';
    .say for @items;
}
```

Hashes also allow celebrating slurpy parameters:

```
dump(alpha => 'a', beta => 'b'); # Prints:
                                 # alpha = a
                                 # beta = b

sub dump(*%data) {
```

```
    for %data.kv {say "$^a = $^b"}
}
```

Notice that the code does not compile if you omit the star in the function signature, as Raku expects exactly what is announced:

```
Too few positionals passed; expected 1 argument but got 0
```

Slurpy-slurpy

The **@ is also working but notice the difference when you pass arrays and lists.

With a single star:

```
my @a = < chocolade ipad >;
my @b = < camelia raku >;

all-together(@a, @b);
all-together(['chocolade', 'ipad'], ['camelia', 'raku']);
all-together(< chocolade ipad >, < camelia raku >);

sub all-together(*@items) {
    .say for @items;
}
```

Currently, each gift is printed on a separate line regardless the way the argument list was passed.

With a double star:

```
keep-groupped(@a, @b);
keep-groupped(['chocolade', 'ipad'], ['camelia', 'camel']);
keep-groupped(< chocolade ipad >, < camelia camel >);

sub keep-groupped(**@items) {
```

```
        .say for @items;
    }
```

This time, the @items array gets two elements only, reflecting the structural types of the arguments:

```
    [chocolade ipad]
    [camelia raku]
```

or

```
    (chocolade ipad)
    (camelia raku)
```

Twigil for dynamic scope

The * twigil, which introduces dynamic scope. It is easy to confuse dynamic variables with global variables but examine the following code.

```
    sub happy-new-year() {
        "Happy new $*year year!"
    }

    my $*year = 2020;
    say happy-new-year();
```

If you omit the star, the code cannot be run:

```
    Variable '$year' is not declared
```

The only way to make it correct is to move the definition of $year above the function definition. With the dynamic variable $*year, the place *where the function is called* defines the result. The $*year variable is not visible in the outer scope of the sub, but it is quite visible in the dynamic scope.

For a dynamic variable, it is not important whether you assign a new value
to an existing variable or create a new one:

```
sub happy-new-year() {
    "Happy new $*year year!"
}


my $*year = 2018;


say happy-new-year();       # 2018


{
    $*year = 2019;          # New value
    say happy-new-year(); # 2019
}


{
    my $*year = 2020;       # New variable
    say happy-new-year(); # 2020
}


say happy-new-year();       # 2019
```

Compiler variables

A number of dynamic pseudo-constants come with Raku, for example:

```
say @*ARGS;         # Prints command-line arguments
say %*ENV<HOME>; # Prints home directory
```

All methods named as this

The .* postfix pseudo-operator calls all the methods with the given name,
which can be found for the given object, and returns a list of results. In the
trivial case you get a scholastically absurd code:

```
> pi.gist.say
3.141592653589793

> pi.*gist.say
(3.141592653589793 3.141592653589793e0)
```

The real power of the `.*` postfix comes with inheritance. It helps to reveal the truth sometimes:

```
class Present {
    method giver() {
        'parents'
    }
}

class ChristmasPresent is Present {
    method giver() {
        'Santa Claus'
    }
}

my ChristmasPresent $present;

$present.giver.say;              # Santa Claus
$present.*giver.join(', ').say; # Santa Claus, parents
```

Just a star but what a difference!

* * *

Now, to the most mysterious part of the star corner of Raku. The next two concepts, the `Whatever` and the `WhateverCode` classes, are easy to mix up with each other. Let's try to do it right.

Whatever

A single * can represent `Whatever`. `Whatever` is a predefined class, which introduces some prescribed behaviour in a few useful cases.

For example, in ranges and sequences, the final * means infinity. We've seen such examples already. Here is another one:

```
.say for 1 .. *;
```

This one-liner has a really high energy conversion efficiency as it generates an infinite list of increasing integers. Press `Ctrl+C` when you are ready to move on.

The range `1 .. *` is the same as `1 .. Inf`.

Returning to our more practical problems, let's create our own class that makes use of the whatever symbol *. Here is a simple example of a class with a multi-method taking either an `Int` value or a `Whatever`.

```
class N {
    multi method display(Int $n) {
        say $n;
    }

    multi method display(Whatever) {
        say 2000 + 100.rand.Int;
    }
}
```

In the first case, the method simply prints the value. The second method prints a random number between 2000 and 2100 instead. As the only argument of the second method is `Whatever`, no variable is needed in the signature.

Here is how you use the class:

```
my $n = N.new;

$n.display(2020);
$n.display(*);
```

The first call echoes its argument, while the second one prints something random.

The Whatever symbol can be held as a bare Whatever. Say, you create an echo function and pass the * to it:

```
sub echo($x) {
    say $x;
}

echo(2018); # 2018
echo(*);    # *
```

This time, no magic happens, the program prints a star.

And now we are at a point where a tiny thing changes a lot.

WhateverCode

Finally, it's time to talk about WhateverCode.

Take an array and print the last element of it. You can't do it by type something like @a[-1], as it generates an error:

```
Unsupported use of a negative -1 subscript
to index from the end; in Raku please
use a function such as *-1
```

The compiler suggests using a `function` such as `*-1`. Is it a function? Yes, more precisely, a `WhateverCode` block:

```
say (*-1).WHAT; # (WhateverCode)
```

Now, print the second half of an array:

```
my @a = < one two three four five six >;
say @a[3..*]; # (four five six)
```

An array is indexed with the range `3..*`. The `Whatever` star as the right end of the range instructs to take all the rest from the array. The type of `3..*` is a `Range`:

```
say (3..*).WHAT; # (Range)
```

Finally, take one element less. We've already seen that to specify the last element, a function such as `*-1` must be used. The same can be done at the right end of a range:

```
say @a[3 .. *-2]; # (four five)
```

At this point, the so-called `Whatever`-currying happens, and a `Range` becomes a `WhateverCode`:

```
say (3 .. *-2).WHAT; # (WhateverCode)
```

`WhateverCode` is a built-in class name; it can easily be used for method dispatching. Let's update the code from the previous section and add a method variant that expects a `WhateverCode` argument:

```
class N {
    multi method display(Int $n) {
        say $n;
    }

    multi method display(Whatever) {
```

```
        say 2000 + 100.rand.Int;
    }

    multi method display(WhateverCode $code) {
        say $code(2000 + 100.rand.Int);
    }
}
```

Now, the star in the argument list falls into either `display(Whatever)` or `display(WhateverCode)`:

```
N.display(2018);        # display(Int $n)
N.display(*);           # display(Whatever)
N.display(* / 2);       # display(WhateverCode $code)
N.display(* - 1000);    # display(WhateverCode $code)
```

Once again, look at the signature of the `display` method:

```
multi method display(WhateverCode $code)
```

The `$code` argument is used as a function reference inside the method:

```
say $code(2000 + 100.rand.Int);
```

The function takes an argument but where is it going to? Or, in other words, what and where is the function body? We called the method as `N.display(* / 2)` or `N.display(* - 1000)`. The answer is that both `* / 2` and `* - 1000` are functions! Remember the compiler's hint about using a `function such as *-1`?

The star here becomes the first function argument, and thus `* / 2` is equivalent to `{$^a / 2}`, while `* - 1000` is equivalent to `{$^a - 1000}`.

Does it mean that `$^b` can be used next to `$^a`? Sure! Make a `WhateverCode` block accept two arguments. How do you indicate the second of them? Not a surprise, with another star! Let us add the fourth variant of the `display` method to our class:

```
multi method display(WhateverCode $code
                        where {$code.arity == 2}) {
    say $code(2000, 100.rand.Int);
}
```

Here, the `where` block is used to narrow the dispatching down to select only those `WhateverCode` blocks that have two arguments. Having this done, two snowflakes are allowed in the method call:

```
N.display( * + * );
N.display( * - * );
```

The calls define the function `$code` that is used to calculate the result. So, the actual operation behind the `N.display( * + * )` is the following: `2000 + 100.rand.Int`.

Need more snow? Add more stars:

```
N.display( * * * );
N.display( * ** * );
```

Similarly, the actual calculations inside are:

```
2000 * 100.rand.Int
```

and

```
2000 ** 100.rand.Int
```

Congratulations! You can now parse the * ** * construct as effortlessly as the compiler does it.

Homework

Let's make an exercise and answer the following question: What does each star mean in the following code?

```
my @n = ((0, 1, * + * ... *).grep: *.is-prime).map: * * * * *;
.say for @n[^5];
```

D'oh. I suggest we start transforming the code to get rid of all the stars and to use a different syntax.

The * after the sequence operator ... means generating the sequence infinitely, so replace it with `Inf`:

```
((0, 1, * + * ... Inf).grep: *.is-prime).map: * * * * *
```

The two stars * + * in the generator function can be replaced with a lambda function with two explicit arguments:

```
((0, 1, -> $x, $y {$x + $y} ... Inf).grep:
    *.is-prime).map: * * * * *
```

Now, a simple syntax alternation. Replace the `.grep:` with a method call with parentheses. Its argument `*.is-prime` becomes a code block, and the star is replaced with the default variable `$_`. Notice that no curly braces were needed while the code was using a `*`:

```
(0, 1, -> $x, $y {$x + $y} ... Inf).grep({
    $_.is-prime
}).map: * * * * *
```

Finally, the same trick for `.map:` but this time there are three arguments for this method, thus, you can write `{$^a * $^b * $^c}` instead of * * * * *, and here's the new layout of the complete program:

```
my @n = (0, 1, -> $x, $y {$x + $y} ... Inf).grep({
        $_.is-prime
    }).map({
        $^a * $^b * $^c
    });
.say for @n[^5];
```

Now it is obvious that the code prints five products of the groups of three prime Fibonacci numbers.

Additional assignments

In textbooks, the most challenging tasks are marked with a *. Here are a couple of them for you to solve yourself.

1. What is the difference between `chdir('/')` and `&*chdir('/')`?
2. Explain the following code and modify it to demonstrate its advantages: `.say for 1...**`.

The EVAL routine

The EVAL routine compiles and executes the code that it gets as an argument.

1

Let us start with evaluating a simple program:

```
EVAL('say 123');
```

This program says 123, there's no surprise here.

2

There are, though, more complicated cases. What, do you think, does the following program print?

```
EVAL('say {456}');
```

I guess it prints not what you expected:

```
-> ;; $_? is raw { #`(Block|140570649867712) ... }
```

It parses the content between the curly braces as a pointy block.

3

What if you try double quotes?

```
EVAL("say {789}");
```

Now it even refuses to compile:

```
===SORRY!=== Error while compiling eval.pl

EVAL is a very dangerous function!!! (use the MONKEY-SEE-NO-
EVAL pragma to override this error,
but only if you're VERY sure your data contains no injection
attacks)
at eval.raku:6
------> EVAL("say {789}") ⏏;
```

4

We can fix the code by adding a few magic words:

```
use MONKEY-SEE-NO-EVAL;

EVAL("say {789}");
```

This time, it prints 789.

5

The code is executed (we don't know yet when exactly, that is the topic of
tomorrow's post), so you can make some calculations, for example:

```
use MONKEY-SEE-NO-EVAL;

EVAL("say {7 / 8 + 9}"); # 9.875
```

6

Finally, if you try passing a code block directly, you cannot achieve the goal
again, even with a blind monkey:

```
use MONKEY-SEE-NO-EVAL;

EVAL {say 123};
```

The error happens at runtime:

```
Constraint type check failed in binding to parameter '$code';
expected anonymous constraint to be met but got
-> ;; $_? is raw { #`...
   in block <unit> at eval.raku line 10
```

This message looks cryptic, but at least we see once again that we got an anonymous pointy block passed to the function.

7

And before we wrap up, an attempt to use a lowercase function name:

```
eval('say 42');
```

There is no such function in Raku, and we get a standard error message:

```
===SORRY!=== Error while compiling eval2.raku
Undeclared routine:
    eval used at line 5. Did you mean 'EVAL', 'val'?
```

Chapter 7
Raku Golf

In the Golf programming contents, you are trying to solve a problem using as few characters as possible. The shortest program wins.

The first test

Let us play Golf and print all prime numbers below 100.

My solution, which needs 22 characters, is the following:

```
.is-prime&&.say for ^C
```

There is no shorter solution in Raku, while in the J programming language, they managed to have only 11 characters. In Raku, eight characters are consumed by the method name already. I believe, to win all Golf contests, you need a special language with very short names (which J is) and a set of built-in routines to generate lists of prime, or Fibonacci, or any other numeric sequence. It should also strongly utilise the Unicode character space.

In our Raku example, there is also a Unicode character, C. This not a simple C, the third letter of the Latin alphabet, but a Unicode character ROMAN NUMERAL ONE HUNDRED (which was originally the third letter of the Latin alphabet, of course). Using this symbol let us saving two characters in the solution.

The **&&** trick is possible because the second part of the Boolean expression is not executed if the first operand is **False**. Notice that you cannot use a single **&** here. The full non-optimised version of the code would require additional spaces and would look like this:

```
.say if .is-prime for ^100
```

The second test

Let's solve another Golf task and print the first 30 Fibonacci numbers, one at a line. We have to use as few characters in the code as possible.

The first approach is rather wordy (even when using `^31` instead of `0..30`, it needs 33 characters):

```
.say for (0, 1, * + * ... *)[^31]
```

There is some room that allows compression. Of course, the first and the most obvious thing is to remove spaces (remaining 28 characters):

```
.say for (0,1,*+*...*)[^31]
```

Another interesting trick is to use the `>>` meta-operator to call the `say` method on each element of the sequence. It compresses the code further to 24 characters:

```
(0,1,*+*...*)[^31]>>.say
```

At this moment, we can employ some Unicode, and gain three more characters (21 left):

```
(0,1,*+*…*)[^31]».say
```

Looks compact already, but there are still some options to try. Let us get rid of the explicit slicing, and try to stop the sequence at the last element:

```
(0,1,*+*…*>514229)».say
```

The code became longer (23 characters), but we do not need an exact number 514 229 here. It is enough to give some close number, which is bigger than the 29th and smaller than the 30th element of the sequence. For example, it can be 823 543, which is 7 powered 7. Write it down using superscripts (19 characters):

```
(0,1,*+*…*>7⁷)».say
```

Finally, it is possible to make it one character less by using another Unicode character representing 800 000 in a single character. Not every (if any) font can display something visually attractive, but Raku takes the character with no complains:

```
(0,1,*+*…*>􏿿)».say
```

These **18 characters** is one character longer than the top result at the code-golf.io site. I have a feeling that you could gain another character by replacing the first two elements of the sequence with ^2, but that does not work in current Rakudo, and you have to return a character to flatten the list: |^2, which makes the solution 18 characters long again.

The desire is to remove the *> part in the condition to stop the sequence and replace it with a fixed number. Unfortunately, there's no way to express 832 040 with powers of the numbers between 1 and 90. Would that be possible, we could use a superscript to calculate the number.

Another idea is to use a regex, but we need at least four characters here, which does not help:

```
(0,1,*+*…/20/)».say
```

But let me stop here and let you to think about it further.

Tips and ideas for the Raku Golf code

Omitting semicolons

Semicolons are not needed at the end of the statement before the end of the program or the end of a code block.

```
say 42;̶
```

Omitting topic variable

If a method is called on the topic variable $_, then the name of the variable is not really needed for Raku to understand what you are talking about, so, avoid explicitly naming the topic variable:

```
$̶_̶.say for 1..10
```

Using postfix forms

In many cases, a single operation can be equally expresses as a code block or as a single operation with a posfix form of the loop or condition. Postfix forms are usually shorter. For example:

```
f̶o̶r̶ ̶1̶.̶.̶1̶0̶ ̶{̶.̶s̶a̶y̶}̶
```

```
.say for 1..10
```

Using ranges for making loops

Ranges are great things to express loop details: in a few characters, you specify both the initial and the final state of the loop variable.

```
.̶s̶a̶y̶ ̶f̶o̶r̶ ̶1̶.̶.̶1̶0̶
```

But think if you can count from 0, in which case, a caret character can be used to get a range starting from 0. The following code prints the numbers 0 to 9:

```
.say for ^10
```

Choosing between a range and a sequence

In loops, sequences can work exactly the same way a range would do. The choice may depend on whether the Golf software counts bytes or Unicode characters. In the first case, the two dots of a range are preferable over the three dots of a range. In the second case, use a Unicode character:

```
.say for 1..10
```

```
.say for 1...10
```

```
.say for 1…10
```

When you need to count downwards, sequences are your friends, as they can deduce the direction of changing the loop counter:

```
.say for 10…1
```

Using map instead of a loop

In some cases, especially when you have to make more than one action with the loop variable, try using map to iterate over all the values:

```
(^10).map: *.say
```

Omitting parentheses and quotes

Raku does not force you to use parentheses in condition checks in the regular form:

```
if ($x > 0) {say $x;exit}
```

Sometimes, you will want to omit parentheses in function or method calls,
too:

```
say(42)
```

```
say 42
```

Neither you need parentheses when declaring arrays or hashes. With arrays,
use the quoting construct on top of that to avoid the quotation marks:

```
my @a = ('alpha', 'beta')
```

```
my @b=<alpha beta>
```

Using chained comparisons

Another interesting feature is using more than one condition in a single expression:

```
say $z if $x < 10 < $y
```

Choosing between methods and functions

In many cases, you can choose between calling a function and using a
method. Method calls can be additionally chained after each other, so you
can save a lot of parentheses or spaces:

```
(^10).map({.sin}).grep: *>0
```

When there exist both a method and a stand-alone function, method call is
often shorter or at least the same length if you omit parentheses.

```
abs($x)
abs $x
$x.abs
```

Using Unicode characters

Operators often have their Unicode equivalents, and you can express a wordy construct with a single character. Compare:

```
if $x=~=$y
```

```
if $x≅$y
```

Built-in constants are also available in the Unicode space, for example, `pi` vs π, or `Inf` vs ∞.

There are many numbers, both small and big, that can be replaced with a single Unicode symbol: `1/3` vs ⅓, or `20` vs ⑳, or `100` vs Ⅽ.

Using superscripts

Superscripts are great for calculating powers. Compare:

```
say $x**2
```

```
$x².say
```

Using \ to make sigilless variables

Don't forget about the following way of binding containers and creating a kind of a sigilless variable:

```
my \a=42;say a
```

Using default parameters

When you are working with functions or class methods, check if there are default values in their signatures. Also check if there is an alternative variant with positional arguments. Compare, for example, three ways of creating a date object.

```
Date.new(year=>2019,month=>1,day=>1)
```

```
Date.new(year=>2019)
```

```
Date.new(2019,1,1)
```

Using && instead of if

Boolean expressions can save a few characters, as Raku will not calculate the second condition if the first gives the result already. For example:

```
.say if $x>0
```

```
$x>0&&.say
```

Choosing between put and say

Finally, sometimes it is better to use put instead of say. In some cases, you will be free from parentheses in the output when printing arrays, for example. In some other cases you will get all values instead of concise output when working with ranges, for example:

```
> say 1..10
1..10

> put 1..10
1 2 3 4 5 6 7 8 9 10
```

Appendix on Compiler Internals

What's behind 0.1 + 0.2

Today, we will examine a one-liner that computes a zero.

```
say 0.1 + 0.2 - 0.3
```

If you are familiar with programming, you know well that as soon as you start using floating-point arithmetic, you lose precision, and you can face the small errors very quickly.

You might also saw the website 0.30000000000000004.com that has a long list of different programming languages and how they print a simple expression `0.1 + 0.2`. In most cases, you don't get an exact value of 0.3. And often when you get it, it is actually the result of rounding during the print operation.

In Raku, 0.1 + 0.2 is *exactly* 0.3, and the above-mentioned one-liner prints an exact zero.

Let us dive a bit into the compiler internals to see how that works. The Grammar of Raku (implemented in the Rakudo compiler) has the following fragment that detects numbers:

```
token numish {
    [
    | 'NaN' >>
    | <integer>
    | <dec_number>
    | <rad_number>
    | <rat_number>
    | <complex_number>
    | 'Inf' >>
    | $<uinf>='∞'
    | <unum=:No+:Nl>
```

```
    ]
}
```

Most likely, you are familiar enough with Raku, and you know that the above behaviour is explained by the fact that it uses rational numbers to store floating-point numbers such as 0.1. That's right, but looking at the grammar, you can see that the journey is a bit longer.

What is called `rat_number` in the grammar is a number written in angle brackets:

```
token rat_number { '<' <bare_rat_number> '>' }
token bare_rat_number {
    <?before <.[--+0..9<>:boxd]>+? '/'>
    <nu=.signed-integer> '/' <de=integer>
}
```

So, if you change the program to:

```
say <1/10> + <2/10> - <3/10>
```

then you will immediately be operating rational numbers. Here is a corresponding action that converts numbers in this format:

```
method rat_number($/) { make $<bare_rat_number>.ast }

method bare_rat_number($/) {
    my $nu := $<nu>.ast.compile_time_value;
    my $de := $<de>.ast;
    my $ast := $*W.add_constant(
        'Rat', 'type_new', $nu, $de, :nocache(1));
    $ast.node($/);
    make $ast;
}
```

At some point, the abstract syntax tree gets a node containing a constant of the Rat type with the $nu and $de parts as numerator and denominator.

In our example, the numbers written in the form of `0.1` first pass the dec_number token:

```
token dec_number {
    :dba('decimal number')
    [
    | $<coeff> = [ '.' <frac=.decint> ] <escale>?
    | $<coeff> = [ <int=.decint> '.' <frac=.decint> ]
                 <escale>?
    | $<coeff> = [ <int=.decint> ] <escale>
    ]
}
```

The integer and the fractional parts of the number get into the `<int>` and `<frac>` keys of the final Match object. The action method for this grammar token is rather complex. Let me show it to you.

```
method dec_number($/) {
    if $<escale> { # wants a Num
        make $*W.add_numeric_constant: $/, 'Num', ~$/;
    } else { # wants a Rat
        my $Int := $*W.find_symbol(['Int']);
        my $parti;
        my $partf;

        # we build up the number in parts
        if nqp::chars($<int>) {
            $parti := $<int>.ast;
        } else {
            $parti := nqp::box_i(0, $Int);
        }
```

```
        if nqp::chars($<frac>) {
            $partf := nqp::radix_I(
                    10, $<frac>.Str, 0, 4, $Int);

            $parti := nqp::mul_I($parti, $partf[1], $Int);
            $parti := nqp::add_I($parti, $partf[0], $Int);

            $partf := $partf[1];
        } else {
            $partf := nqp::box_i(1, $Int);
        }

        my $ast := $*W.add_constant(
            'Rat', 'type_new', $parti, $partf,
            :nocache(1));
        $ast.node($/);
        make $ast;
    }
}
```

For each of the numbers `0.1`, `0.2`, and `0.3`, the above code takes their integer
and fractional parts, prepares the two integers, `$parti` and `$partf`, and
passes them to the same constructor of a new constant as we saw in the
`rat_number` action, and after that you get a `Rat` number.

Now we skip some details and take a look at another important part of rational numbers that you have to know about.

In our example, the integer and the fractional parts get the following values:

```
$parti=1, $partf=10
$parti=2, $partf=10
$parti=3, $partf=10
```

You can easily see it yourself if you hack on your local copy of Rakudo files.

Alternatively, use the `--target=parse` option in the command line:

```
$ raku --target=parse -e'say 0.1 + 0.2 - 0.3'
```

A part of the output will contain the data we want to see:

```
- 0: 0.1
- value: 0.1
    - number: 0.1
    - numish: 0.1
        - dec_number: 0.1
        - frac: 1
        - int: 0
        - coeff: 0.1
- 1: 0.2
- value: 0.2
    - number: 0.2
    - numish: 0.2
        - dec_number: 0.2
        - coeff: 0.2
        - frac: 2
        - int: 0
```

Having the numbers presented as fractions, it is quite easy to make exact calculations, and that's why we see a pure zero in the output.

Returning to our fractions. If you print both numerator and denominator (using the `nude` method, for example), you will see that the fraction is normalised if possible:

```
> <1/10>.nude.say
(1 10)
> <2/10>.nude.say
(1 5)
> 0.2.nude.say
(1 5)
```

```
> 0.3.nude.say
(3 10)
```

As you see, instead of 2/10 we have 1/5, which represents the same number with the same accuracy. When you use the number, you should not worry about finding the common divider for both fractions, for example:

```
> (0.1 + 0.2).nude.say
(3 10)
```

Afterword

Great to hear that you reached the end of the book. If you came here earlier than you have read the rest of the book, I would recommend you check the Contents and enjoy the Raku examples.

I hope you loved the way Raku can express your ideas in just a few characters of code. Be careful not to go too far and create cryptic programs that are difficult to read.

You can make a significant impact in making Raku a popular programming language. Just start using it bit by bit in your practice and share your experience both online and offline.

Would you like to give your feedback, the author would love to receive it via e-mail: mail@deeptext.media.